Advocacy Awareness Training Workbook

For Professionals Working in

Health and Social Care and Education Settings

HSC Training Link

Copyright © 2017

All rights reserved.

ISBN-13: 978-1542723794

ISBN-10: 1542723795

Index

1. Learning Outcomes
2. Candidate and Manager to complete
3. Learning Outcome 1 - Describe what advocacy is and why it is needed
15. Learning Outcome 2 - Understand the principles of advocacy
26. Learning Outcome 3 - Understand influencing factors and problems in advocacy
38. Learning Outcome 4 - Describe different types of advocacy
49. Learning Outcome 5 - Assess suitability of advocacy provision
56. References
57. Notes

Learning Outcomes

This training workbook will give you a basic understanding of advocacy provision. The learner will work in a health, social care or education environment and requires an awareness of how advocacy can help service users. They will learn about what advocacy is and why it is important, the different types of advocacy and situations in which advocacy may be needed.

Complete this workbook to demonstrate that you can:

1. Describe what advocacy is and why it is needed
2. Understand the principles of advocacy
3. Describe different types of advocacy
4. Understand influencing factors and problems in advocacy
5. Assess suitability of advocacy provision

CANDIDATE DETAILS

Your name:

....

Your signature

....

Place of employment:

....

Date workbook started:

....

Date workbook completed:

....

MANAGER DETAILS

I certify that the candidate named above completed this workbook.

Manager's name:

....

Manager's signature:

....

Date ....

LEARNING OUTCOME 1 - Describe what advocacy is and why it is needed.

To understand how advocacy works, you first need to know what advocacy is.

Definition of Advocacy

"Public support for or recommendation of a particular cause or policy."

"The profession or work of a legal advocate."

(https://en.oxforddictionaries.com/definition/advocacy)

Definition of Advocate

The Merriam Webster dictionary goes into a little more detail when we look at the word 'advocate':

"One that pleads the cause of another; specifically one that pleads the cause of another before a tribunal or judicial court."
"One that defends or maintains a cause or proposal."
"One that supports or promotes the interests of another."

(https://www.merriam-webster.com/dictionary/advocate)

Definition of Independent Advocacy

"Advocacy is taking action to help people say what they want, secure their rights, represent their interests and obtain services they need. Advocates and advocacy providers work in partnership with the people they support and take their side. Advocacy promotes social inclusion, equality and social justice."

(*Advocacy Code of Practice*)

Setting the Scene

Have you ever asked yourself the following questions?

'How would I get my point of view across if I was unable to do so myself?'

'How can I make it easier for people who are unable to put their point of view across?'

Not everyone is able to speak for themselves in all situations. They may have communication problems (for example) or the services they need to interact with may not be very good at listening and responding.

Does Advocacy Matter?

Yes it does. We all have the same right to be heard and the same right to be treated with dignity and respect.

For those that need it, advocacy is essential to wellbeing and helps maintain self-worth; we all need to feel valued as people, no matter what our circumstances are.

Everyone needs to know that their views are important and that they are being listened to. The most vulnerable people in society are those without a 'voice', those that struggle to get themselves heard and those that have little or no understanding that they need someone to speak up for them.

TASK 1

> If someone was to ask you what advocacy is, what would you say to him or her? What does advocacy mean to you personally?

TASK 2

> If someone were to ask you what advocacy is in relation to service provision, what would you say?

People who use services have a diverse range of needs.

Advocacy is important for everyone. It supports our mental health and allows us to express our individualism. Expressing our views or needs can become more difficult as we get older or become less able. Unlike people who have had advocacy support throughout their life, those requiring help at a later time in their lifetime can slip through the net if professionals from health and social care are either not on hand, or miss the opportunity to bring advocacy skills into the way they work.

Advocacy is not just about referring people to an advocacy service.

TASK 3

How would you feel if you were taken ill (for example) and from that point onwards were unable to speak? What sort of things would worry you?

TASK 4

Think about this scenario. You have a parent with early stage dementia, which affects their thinking and reasoning skills. What things would you worry about, on their behalf?

What is Advocacy?

Advocacy services help people – particularly those who are most vulnerable in society – to:

- Access information and services
- Be involved in decisions about their lives
- Explore choices and options
- Defend and promote their rights and responsibilities
- Speak out about issues that matter to them

What is an Advocate?

An *advocacy service* is provided by an *advocate* who is independent of social services and the NHS, and who is not part of a person's family or one of their friends.

An advocate's role includes arguing an individual's case when needed, and making sure the correct procedures are followed by health and social care services.

What Do Advocates Do?

As an advocate is *independent*, it means they are there to represent a person's wishes without giving their personal opinion and without *representing* the views of anyone else. An advocate might help to access information needed or might go with an individual to meetings or interviews in a *supportive role*. They might also write letters on a person's behalf, or speak for them in situations where the person feels they are not able to speak for themselves.

Local Authorities

Each local authority receives funding for advocacy services. Details of advocacy services are available from each individual council.

Benefits of Advocacy

The differences that advocacy interventions make can be broken down into:

- The benefits that arise from the *process* of advocacy itself - i.e. process outcomes
- The *outcome* that that advocacy *achieves*

'Action for Advocacy' defines the practice of advocacy as:

'Taking action to help people say what they want, secure their rights, represent their interests and obtain the services they need.'

(Action for Advocacy website, accessed January 2017)

Impact of Advocacy on People's Outcomes – Research Studies

- People's voices are heard (Stewart et al., 2013).
- People value being listened to by someone who understands their concerns (ODI, 2009a)
- Increased ability to access and use information and services (Roberts et al., 2012)
- Increased ability to make informed decisions and be involved in decision-making
- (Roberts et al., 2012)
- Increased knowledge of and ability to obtain rights and entitlements

(SSCR Advocacy Scoping Review 2014)

Outcomes achieved by advocacy reported include:

- Increased confidence
- Increased choice and control
- Increased independence
- Increased feeling of being safe and secure
- Improved health and wellbeing
- Reduced mental distress
- Empowerment and personal development

TASK 5

Have your views on what advocacy is changed? Describe what advocacy is and why it is needed.

TASK 5 (Continued)

Advocacy Skills - Health and Social Care Professionals

Most professionals working in health or social care will act as advocates in their job role, either on a daily basis or on occasion.

- A social worker or community nurse may need to obtain extra benefits or a particular service for a client
- A housing official may need to help a tenant whose benefit has been delayed thus placing them at risk of homelessness
- A voluntary body may decide to challenge a statement of special educational needs for a child.

Care Act 2014

The Care Act is a law about the care and support of adults and carers. It brings lots of pieces of legislation into one new law.

Local authorities must involve people in decisions made about them and their care and support. No matter how complex a person's needs, local authorities are required to help people express their wishes and feelings, support them in weighing up their options, and assist them in making their own decisions.

The main purpose of the Care Act is to support people to get the outcomes that matter to them in their life. It has to focus on the needs and goals of the person and put them at the centre.

Local authorities must ensure that all adults have access to information and advice on their care and support and must keep them safe from abuse and neglect.

There is an *advocacy duty*. This applies from first contact with the local authority and at any subsequent stage of the assessment, planning, care review, safeguarding enquiry or safeguarding adult review.

If it appears to the authority that a person has care and support needs, then a judgement must be made as to whether that person has substantial difficulty in being involved.

If there is not an appropriate individual to support them, an <u>independent advocate</u> must be appointed to support and represent the person for the purpose of assisting their involvement if these two conditions are met, and if the individual is required to take part in one or more of the following processes described in the Care Act:

- Needs assessment
- Carer's assessment
- Preparation of a care and support or support plan
- Review of a care and support or support plan
- Child's needs assessment
- Child's carer's assessment
- Young carer's assessment
- Safeguarding enquiry
- Safeguarding adult review
- An appeal against a local authority decision under Part 1 of the Care Act (subject to further consultation)

The **appropriate individual** <u>cannot</u> be:

- Already providing care or treatment to the person in a *professional* capacity or on a *paid* basis
- Someone the person *does not want* to support them
- Someone who is unlikely to be able to, or available to, adequately support the person's involvement
- Someone implicated in an enquiry into abuse or neglect or who has been judged by a safeguarding adult review to have failed to prevent abuse or neglect

Differences between the Care Act duties and the Mental Capacity Act duties:

- Under the *Care Act,* the appropriate individual's role is to facilitate the person's involvement.
- Under the *Mental Capacity Act** the role of the IMCA is to consult the person and make decisions on their behalf.

*See Page 31

TASK 6

In your own words, summarise what the Care Act says about advocacy:

LEARNING OUTCOME 2 - Understand the principles of advocacy.

Advocacy has developed and grown into a valuable service for people requiring help. There are a wide range of advocacy models and schemes that have come into being.

The Advocacy Charter (2002)

This gives guidance to advocates and advocacy organisations. The guidance is intended to ensure that the fundamental principles of advocacy are followed.

The Key Principles

- Accessible
- Clear of purpose
- Professional
- Equal in opportunity
- Empowering
- Confidential
- Accountable
- Independent
- Client centred
- Complaints

The Principle of Accessibility

- No monetary charges for eligible people
- Convenient places and times for discussions and meetings
- Accessible meeting places for the service user
- Any information to be given to the service user to be in a format that can be understood

TASK 7

Case Study 1 *Lola is a 37-year-old woman with multiple sclerosis. She lives with her partner Tom and their two children, Bethany aged 3 and Megan aged 7. Tom is signing on as unemployed and has enrolled on a part-time college course. Lola's incapacity affects her in a number of different ways.* What accessibility problems might Lola have?

TASK 8

Case Study 2 *Jack is a 73-year-old man with early stage dementia. He lives with his wife of 50 years, Edna. They have 3 grandchildren. They live in their own home and their daughter calls in on a daily basis. Jack is affected by short-term memory loss.* What accessibility problems might Jack have?

TASK 9

Case Study 3 *Mohammed is a 47-year-old man who is visually impaired. He lives with his wife Salma and their 3 teenage children. Salma has a part-time job and 2 of the children are still at school.* What accessibility problems might |Mohammed have?

Follow up on Case Studies – did you consider the following?

- Is Lola a wheelchair user?
- Can Lola climb stairs?
- Does Lola's MS affect her arms and hands? (Writing)
- Does Lola's MS affect her cognition? (Memory, thought, word recognition)
- Does Lola's MS affect her speech?
- Is Lola able to go out without the help of her husband? (This is not just a mobility issue – she has 2 children, one of which is not yet at school and her husband is attending a part-time college course)
- Can Jack retain all verbal information given to him?
- Can Jack remember appointment arrangements?
- Is Jack happy to leave his wife unattended?
- Does Mohammed's eyesight affect his ability to see and read information?
- Is Mohammed better able to communicate in a language other than English?
- Is Mohammed able to go out without the help of another person?

The Principle of Clarity of Purpose

Advocates should know the extent and limitations of their role - i.e. the areas in which they *can* act and those in which they *cannot*. It is the *duty* of the advocate to *inform* the service user of their *role* before entering into any advocacy arrangements.

There is also a link with the principle of confidentiality. In areas that an advocate cannot act, they must obtain *permission* from the client before referring these matters to other agencies. Clarity of purpose is about:

- Explaining simply what advocacy is
- Explaining simply the benefits of advocacy
- Providing written information and a copy of the Code of Practice if requested

It is vital that service users and advocates know what they can expect from an advocacy service. Providing clarity helps in the following ways:

- Service users can assess the support received
- Advocates know what their role is and the boundaries
- Appropriate referrals can be made, ensuring that funding intended for independent advocacy is used correctly.

The Principle of Independence

- Advocates should be independent from statutory bodies
- There should be no conflicts of interest
- Potential conflicts of interest must be disclosed to the line manager for advice

It is the *independence* of advocacy that allows advocacy services to be led by the service user and consequently responsible to the service user.

Studies show that independence is one of the crucial aspects that people coming to advocacy services are looking for.

The Principle of Empowerment

Advocates should support *self-advocacy* through *empowerment*. Clients should be empowered to make decisions about the *role of the advocate* as well as making personal decisions. Empowerment is about supporting people to develop new skills and the confidence to speak for themselves.

Advocacy is about increasing the amount of *control* that people have over their own lives, advocacy services need to ensure they are working in a way that fosters independence.

What is Empowerment?

- Client encouraged to make decisions to take control of their lives
- A process building self-esteem
- A process building confidence
- Gives power to clients

What is Empowerment?

- **The importance of sharing information:**
- Enables client to make informed choices
- **The importance of effective communication:**
- Ensures clients and service users are empowered

The Principle of Equal Opportunity

Advocates must have a firm knowledge of equal opportunities. The Equality Act is the key piece of legislation protecting the rights of equal opportunity.

Part of the Equality Act is the *Public Sector Equality Duty.*

What is the Equality Duty?

- A duty on all public bodies and others carrying out public functions to take account of:
  - Equality
  - Discrimination
  - Good relations
- Between protected groups - in the way that:
  - Policies are drawn up
  - Services are delivered
  - Goods and services are purchased
  - People are employed

Other Organisations

- The general duty also applies to:
  - Other organisations when carrying out public functions
  - Voluntary or private organisations if carrying out public functions on behalf of public bodies
- E.g.:
- A private care home receiving local authority funding for a client
  - The general duty applies to services provided to that client

Advocacy services and all advocates must understand and work within all legislation and policies regarding equal opportunities and should be pro-active in challenging and addressing all matters of inequality, discrimination and social exclusion. **They should therefore receive training in all these matters.**

Equal opportunity includes respecting religious, cultural and spiritual needs.

The Principle of Putting People First

This is about putting the client at the centre – a person centred approach.

- Advocates should ensure that the wishes and interests of the client always comes first
- Advocates should not withhold information from the client
- Advocates should be non-judgmental and respectful of peoples' needs, views and experiences

The Principle of Confidentiality

Advocates must work within the legislation and policies regarding confidentiality of information. All services must have a confidentiality policy.

All information must be kept confidential, unless it is *legally acceptable* to disclose.

There are strict criteria for disclosure.

There must be full disclosure of the *level* of confidentiality that can be *guaranteed*:

- Explaining conditions under which confidentiality may be breached
- Explaining that discussions take place with a line manager

Confidentiality also means securely storing all written information, but also allowing access to any written information if requested by the service user.

A relationship of *trust* enables service users to talk fully and therefore be then able to explore the options available to them.

The Data Protection Act 1998 tells organisations how they should deal with your personal details if they are on a computer or in writing.

The information should be up-to-date, accurate and relevant. Organisations should also make sure that only certain people can see the information.

The Principle of Training and Support

Advocates must have received:

- Appropriate training
- On-going training and personal development

Support with:

- Reflection and analysis, *and*
- Counselling (if required)

The Principle of Professionalism

The relationship between the advocate and the client must be a professional relationship. It must never go beyond a *professional* relationship.

The Principle of Accountability

Advocacy schemes should have systems for effective monitoring and evaluation of services given.

Advocates should always work within the law and to their organisation's *Code of Practice*.

Accountability also means:

- Keeping accurate and up to date written records
- Keeping clients informed
- Not making promises that cannot be followed through

Complaints

The advocacy provider must have a written policy describing how individuals, including relevant stakeholders, can make complaints or give feedback about the service or about individual advocates. Where necessary, the organisation will enable people who use its services to access external independent support to make or pursue a complaint.

The Principle of Safeguarding

Clear policies and procedures will be in place to ensure safeguarding issues are identified and acted upon. Advocates will be supported to understand the different forms of abuse, neglect, issues relating to confidentiality and what to do if they suspect a client is at risk.

All these principles are for the protection of the client and the advocate.

TASK 10

In your own words, summarise the key principles of advocacy. You could give some examples to demonstrate that you understand each principle.

What does clarity of purpose mean?

TASK 11

What does empowerment mean?

TASK 12

Why is accountability important?

LEARNING OUTCOME 3 - Understand influencing factors and problems in advocacy.

We could all find ourselves in a situation where we lack the capacity in some way to:

- Choose for ourselves, or
- Fully represent our own interests

If we found ourselves in this situation, we would still want to have control of our own lives.

Advocacy is about helping people to say what they want to say and say what they want to happen. Advocacy is about taking action to:

- Secure people's rights
- Represent their interests
- Obtain services needed

Advocacy can help ensure that an individual's views and needs are heard, respected and acted upon.

Advocacy promotes:

- Social inclusion
- Equality
- Social justice
- The protection of vulnerable people
- Individual rights, underpinned within the Care Value Base

Social Exclusion

Individuals and groups can become isolated in society because of a number of factors – for example:

- Unemployment
- Health problems

Advocacy is one way of ensuring that a person's rights and interests are represented.

Equality

The principles of equality are reinforced by various pieces of legislation. Promoting anti-discriminatory practices will ensure:

- A right to access to services
- A right to non-discriminatory medical treatment

Social Justice

Advocacy is one way of ensuring fairness within society. This is closely linked to equality.

The Protection of Vulnerable People

The most vulnerable groups in society are often not able to protect themselves from:

- Verbal abuse
- Physical abuse
- Neglect
- Emotional abuse

Advocacy not only provides practical help but also can play a positive and vital role in:

- Preventing abuse
- Identifying abuse

Individual Rights

Service users and potential service users have rights.

The Care Value Base is a set of principles that applies to all health and social care settings and individual workers.

Devised by the Care Sector Consortium in 1992, it forms the basis of all ethical decisions and judgments made in health and social care.

Care Value Base

This is a set of principles to be used in all dealings with clients, service users and service providers (and by service providers).

It is a duty, providing the basis for all care provision.

1. Respecting a person's identity
    - Even if this doesn't 'fit' with your own beliefs/values
    - This means recognising and accepting the diversity of people whilst ensuring equality for all
2. Maintaining confidentiality in all dealings
3. Communicating effectively at all times

4. Fostering communication as a two-way process
5. Everyone is entitled to choice
6. Everyone has a right to dignity
7. Alternative approaches should be part of the way you think, act, advise etc.

TASK 13

Explain why advocacy is important:

TASK 13 (Continued)

Physical Illness

There are many illnesses that can limit a person's ability to say what they want to say or say what they want to happen.

Physical illness can be draining and worrying. Sometimes a person can be so focused on their illness that other areas of their life get into difficulty.

Physical illness has complex causes. The ageing process can result in a breakdown of health and well-being. Social, economic and environmental issues also play a part.

Mental Illness

Mental illness can drastically affect a person's ability to function normally. They can have a sense of hopelessness. They can also behave in different ways.

People with a mental illness may have difficulties with:

- Sleep (affecting daytime activities)
- Decision making
- Concentration
- Forgetfulness

Physical Disability

Some physical disabilities have obvious effects on communication.

- Sensory impairment (sight or hearing)
- Neurological impairments

Others are affected in a less obvious way.

- E.g. poor self-esteem
- E.g. stigmatisation

Capacity

This means the ability to make a decision about a particular issue at the time the decision needs to be made or to give consent to a particular act.

The Mental Capacity Act 2005 gives people:

- Power to influence the type of care they want in the future
- Power to ensure their wishes are carried out

The Act applies to adults and young adults aged 16 and over in England and Wales. It helps people to make their own decisions and protects people who cannot make their own decisions.

The Mental Capacity Act also gives guidance to:

- People who want to help a person to make their own decisions
- People who need to decide whether a person is 'lacking capacity'
- People who need to decide what to do if a person cannot make a decision

What is Mental Capacity?

Mental capacity means being capable of making decisions. Lacking capacity means the inability to make decisions.

Lasting Power of Attorney

A Lasting Power of Attorney (LPA) is a statutory form of power of attorney created by the Mental Capacity Act (2005). Anyone who has the capacity to do so may choose a person (an 'attorney') to take decisions on their behalf if they subsequently lose capacity.

TASK 14

In your own words, what is the Mental Capacity Act 2005 and what does it do?

Mental Capacity

People with mental illnesses and disabilities can often be (wrongly) considered 'not capable' of making their own decisions.

The *Mental Incapacity Act (2005)* has made clear the situation regarding competence.

It also introduced changes to help people make their own decisions and protect those that cannot.

The Key to Success

A recent review of advocacy for people who use social care services revealed that there is a lack of understanding about the evidence base around the impact of advocacy in social care, and an absence of an authoritative source that seeks to bring this information together in one, understandable place.

At the same time, there seems to be a lack of shared understanding about what advocacy is and is not, with limited understanding about the different role and functions of varying types of advocacy – such as self-advocacy and professional advocacy (types of advocacy will be looked at in the next learning outcome). These findings are mentioned here as part of influencing factors and problems' (National Institute for Health Research, School for Social Care Research, NHS).

Problems - What Advocacy is Not?

There are a number of things that advocacy is not. For example, it is not (Salman, 2012):

- Information or advice – these are separate and distinct from advocacy
- About mediation, counselling, befriending, taking complaints or giving advice, although elements of these can be found to varying degrees across the different models
- Support from staff – advocacy is independent from the delivery of direct services
- Support from relatives

Other Influencing Factors

Demand for advocacy services has grown.

62% of advocacy services who replied to an Action for Advocacy survey reported that demand had increased for their services in the last 12 months, typically by between 10 to 40%. This increase was felt to reflect the changes in welfare benefits and health and social care services, as well as increasing debt and financial problems (Action for Advocacy, 2011).

Advocacy also plays an essential role in preventing, detecting and responding to abuse. The importance of people's voices being heard, and advocacy's role in this, have been highlighted by reviews about, for example, Winterbourne View private hospital (Flynn, 2012), the Confidential Inquiry into premature deaths of people with learning disabilities (Heslop et al., 2013) and the Francis Inquiry into Mid-Staffordshire NHS Foundation Trust (Francis, 2013).

The Advocacy Consortium UK (2009) estimated that there are over 1,000 independent advocacy organisations in the UK providing various forms of independent advocacy, using both paid staff and volunteers. However, there is patchy geographical provision (ODI, 2009).

The impact of funding cuts in the current economic climate also affects services. Action for Advocacy's 2011 survey found:

- The support of fewer people – 74% of advocacy providers who responded to Action for Advocacy's survey said their funding was insufficient to cover current demand, and 63% said they expected to support fewer people in the future

- The making advocates or associated staff redundant (39%)

- The reduction of service hours or operating waiting lists (45%)

TASK 15

In your own words, describe influencing factors and problems in advocacy:

TASK 15 (Continued)

In your own words, describe influencing factors and problems in advocacy:

LEARNING OUTCOME 4 - Describe different types of advocacy.

Who needs advocacy?

Anyone who needs support to:

- Make changes and take control of their life
- Be valued and included in their community
- Be listened to and understood.

A person accessing advocacy could, for example, be someone with a learning difficulty or an older person who has dementia.

Advocacy is about helping people to:

- Say what they want to say
- Say what they want to happen

All people are very different from each other. Their needs for support are different, and may change during their life. A range of advocacy services and types has developed to recognise these differences.

The different types of advocacy include:

- Self-Advocacy
- Group Advocacy

- Peer Advocacy
- Citizen Advocacy
- Professional Advocacy
- Non-Instructed Advocacy

These types of advocacy services can be provided via:

1. Individual advocates, *or*
2. Advocacy schemes

Advocates <u>all</u> work in partnership with the people they support and take their side.

All advocacy types are of equal importance. The type of advocacy used should depend on what is best suited to the person who needs it. The same person may need different types of advocacy support at different times in their life.

Common to all types of advocacy is that the process should be person-centred. The person should always be at the centre of the advocacy process:

- What that person wants and finding the best way of letting the people who need to know this information

Citizen advocate

- This is an unpaid member of the local community, independent of service providers and families - for example, a member of a support group
- The advocacy relationship is based on trust and confidentiality
- A one-to-one advocacy partnership
- A citizen advocate identifies choices and decisions, but does not make or influence them
- A long term partnership, not time limited , continues for as long as both partners want it to

The aims are to involve people in their local community by enabling them to have a voice and to make decisions about the things that affect their lives.

Citizen advocacy partnerships are long term and last for as long as the citizen advocate and the individual want them. They usually operate with support from a coordinated scheme.

Citizen advocates are volunteers who develop long-term relationships with people and speak up for them.

Volunteer advocate

Most organisations and schemes use volunteers to deliver some aspects of the services they provide. Advocacy 'schemes' also use volunteers for some aspects of advocacy.

Volunteers receive induction and training, ongoing support and regular supervision.

- The focus is on <u>specific</u> tasks

Legal Advocates

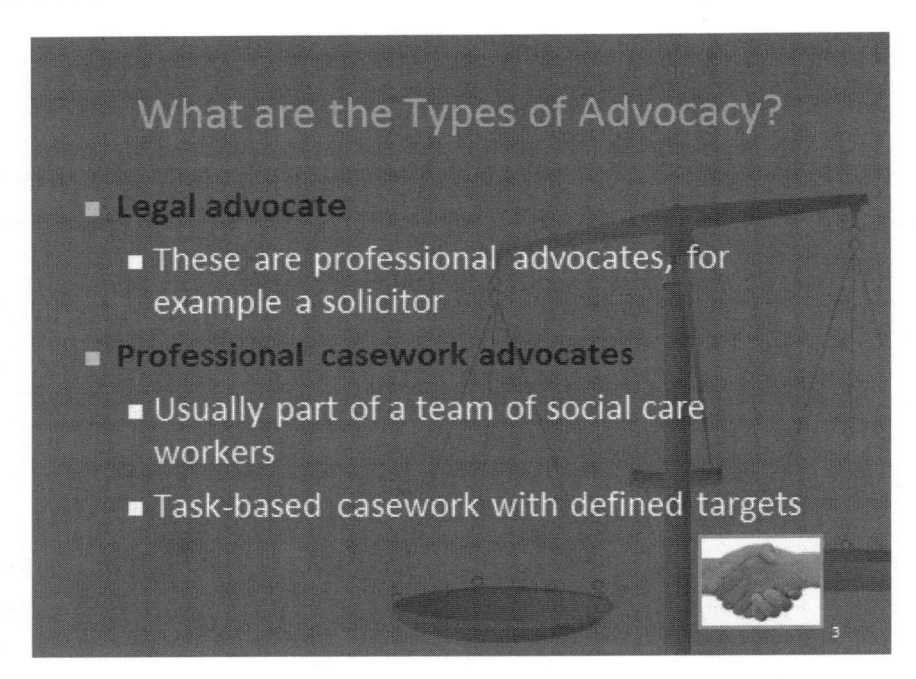

What are the Types of Advocacy?

- Legal advocate
  - These are professional advocates, for example a solicitor
- Professional casework advocates
  - Usually part of a team of social care workers
  - Task-based casework with defined targets

> ## What are the Types of Advocacy?
>
> - **Self advocate**
>   - Someone representing themselves
> - **Formal advocates**
>   - Schemes set up by volunteer or support groups
>   - Usually managed by a voluntary service provider
>   E.g. Age UK, Mind, Scope

Peer Advocacy

When people share similar experiences, a 'peer' advocate can be very beneficial. For example-shared experiences of living in care or mental health issues. There are many peer advocates with a learning disability.

Self-Advocacy

Self-advocacy is about taking control of decisions and telling others what you want. It enables people to speak up for themselves. It is the best kind of advocacy, provided people feel able and willing to do so.

Self-advocacy groups are a good way of encouraging this. Self-advocacy groups are often groups of people who use services or have the same interests locally. They work together to make sure they have a say in how those services are run. They are a very good way for people to support each other and they can help to build confidence so that people feel more able to speak up for themselves.

Case Advocacy

These are forms of advocacy similar to citizen advocacy, but which focus on one issue or set of issues. Case advocacy can run together with peer, citizen, or self-advocacy to give extra support in dealing with a particular problem. The support may be needed because a lot of work needs to be done, because of a break down in an advocacy partnership, or because issues requiring special expertise arise, e.g. in law, child protection, education, housing, employment, and financial matters.

Statutory Advocacy

Mental Capacity Advocacy Service

This service helps with matters involving health services, care services, social services and housing departments.

E.g.:

- Medical treatment decisions
- Going into hospital
- Going into a care home

The Mental Capacity Act 2005 provides a statutory framework for acting and making decisions on behalf of individuals who lack the mental capacity to do so for themselves. The independent Mental Capacity advocate (IMCA) service supports people who lack capacity and who have no family or friends to support them when serious decisions are taken in their lives.

Mental Health Advocates (IMHA)

The Mental Health Act 2007 made provision for independent Mental Health Advocates (IMHA) for 'qualifying' patients in England.

TASK 16

Summarise in your own words, different types of advocacy:

CASE STUDY

Syd and Patricia's story - service used: Older Carers Advocacy

Now in their 80s, Syd and Patricia have been in touch with our Older Carers Advocacy Service since it was launched. Their son, Colin, has been registered blind since birth and has learning difficulties. Now 54, Colin has trouble walking and is diabetic. In recent years, he has been diagnosed with cancer - twice.

"The support we've had from the Older Carers Advocacy Service has been amazing. Anne, our advocate, is a rock. If we have any problems ourselves or need help with any aspect of Colin's care, we get in touch and Anne will help us to sort things out. If she doesn't know the answer immediately she will always take the time to find out!"

With Anne's support, Syd and Patricia have each had a carer's assessment and for the first time the couple, have access to a social worker and are receiving a respite care budget. With Anne's support, a personalised budget has been arranged for Colin and his parents have been able to think positively about what will happen when they can no longer give him the care he needs. By working with Anne to complete a FuturePlan which details their views and wishes with regard to Colin's care in an emergency or crisis situation, the whole family now feel confident that Colin will be properly looked after and that going into a care home is not the only option for him.

"The most important thing for us has been having someone we can talk to who really cares about our needs. We aren't just given instructions and handed leaflets and left to get on with it ourselves. The Older Cares Advocacy Service is there to actually support you to sort out and resolve the issues or concerns you have. It is the best thing that has ever happened to us."

Source: http://www.seap.org.uk/case-studies/syd-and-patricias-story.html

Accessed: 11.55 22/01/2017

CASE STUDY

Peter and Maisie's story - service used: Older Carers Advocacy

Peter, aged 79 and Maisie, aged 81 care for Masie's adult son Richard who has Downs Syndrome. They have been attending the Older Carers Advocacy Service 'Tea and Cake' support sessions and have received support to complete a Future Plan that outlines Richard's care needs and preferences and details their wishes for his care when they are no longer able to look after him as they do now. But it was Older Carers Advocate Anne's determination to ensure Peter received the benefits he was entitled to that made them realise what the support of the Older Carers Advocacy Service could help them achieve.

Whilst talking to Anne, Maisie explained that she received Carers Premium and that she was also in receipt of an Attendance Allowance due to her own ill-health. When Anne enquired whether Peter also claimed Carers Premium for caring for his wife, the answer was an emphatic 'no' - they did not believe he was entitled to. Through her experience of working with carers, Anne was aware that many carers do not claim this benefit, but are often entitled to it.

Pensioners who receive a State Pension cannot also receive Carers Allowance, but if they meet all the criteria for Carers Allowance they have what is known as 'underlying entitlement' and may qualify for Carers Premium which gives them additional funds of around £31 per week. Anne felt sure that Peter would qualify for Carers Premium and agreed that she would make some initial enquiries to the Pensions Office.

Then followed an incredible series of events where the pensions people said 'yes, he did qualify' and then 'no, he doesn't qualify' and then 'you need to fill out a form' and then 'yes' and 'no' again. Eventually they agreed that Peter did qualify due to the 'underlying entitlement' condition - just as Anne had suspected. Without advocacy support from the Older Carers Advocacy Service and Anne's valuable experience, he wouldn't have received a penny.

Source: http://www.seap.org.uk/case-studies/peter-and-maisies-story.html

Accessed 11.58 22/01/2017

CASE STUDY

John's Story - service used: Community Mental Health Advocacy

John contacted seAp because he wanted advocacy support to help him challenge some of the decisions that had been made about his health care. John had been medically discharged from the army following a severe injury, and had been prescribed pain relief which included both anti-inflammatory and anti-depressant medication.

Prison medical staff suddenly reduced his medication, without discussion or explanation which led to unpleasant consequences for John. He wanted help and support to find out why he was no longer receiving the pain relief prescribed by his pain specialist and whether this decision could be reversed. He also wanted to know why the changes had been made without any discussion with him.

In addition, John believed he was suffering from Post Traumatic Stress Disorder (PTSD) but after assessment by the PrimaryMental HealthCare Team (PMHCT) he was refused a referral to the mental health in-reach team. He wanted to try to overturn this decision with our support.

Working with clients in prison settings can be very challenging due to the severe restrictions on communication with prisoners and the often poor communication between prison staff and external agencies. This makes progress very slow and frustrating. Despite these difficulties, our advocate was able to build a relationship with John and the professionals involved in his care and, with perseverance, bring about the outcomes that John was looking for. John's advocate was able to arrange and support him at a meeting with his GP where all the issues concerning John were discussed.

As a result of this meeting and a series of follow-up calls undertaken by his advocate, John's medication was improved and he was given access to psychiatric services for diagnosis and treatment of his PTSD. John was very happy with the support he received from seAp and wouldn't hesitate to recommend our service to other prisoners.

Source: http://www.seap.org.uk/case-studies/johns-story.html

Accessed 12.02 22/01/2017

TASK 17– Questions and Answers

A person with dementia needs an IMCA not an advocate	Yes/No
A person with a learning disability cannot be an advocate	Yes/No

TASK 18

Liaise with your line manager. This about an (anonymous) service user known to you and identify and area in which an advocate may be required. Record your thoughts as a case study here:

TASK 18 (continued)

LEARNING OUTCOME 5 - Assess suitability of advocacy provision.

There are many different organisations offering advocacy services.

Some advocacy services help people with a specific condition. For example, *Diabetes UK* offers an advocacy service for vulnerable people with diabetes.

Age UK gives advice and information to older people and their carers, family, friends and other people involved in their care. Some branches offer advocacy services.

Voiceability specialises in working with vulnerable people, such as those who have a disability, communication difficulties, mental health needs, and those who lack capacity, or those who have no one else to support them.

SEAP is an organisation that provides advocacy support for people with learning or physical disabilities. It also provides training for advocates, volunteers and professionals who need to understand the role of advocacy in health and social care services.

The *British Institute of Learning Disabilities (BILD)* works with people with learning disabilities and their families to make sure they have the right support to make choices and decisions about their own lives.

Mencap's advocacy service enables people with a learning disability to speak up and make decisions about things that are important to them, while their *Empower Me* service provides personalised advocacy support for people with a learning disability. It aims to help people develop the skills, confidence and knowledge needed to voice concerns and secure rights.

Advocacy and Mental Capacity

The *Mental Capacity Act 2005* introduced Independent Mental Capacity Advocates (IMCAs). An IMCA supports people who cannot make or understand decisions by stating their views and wishes or securing their rights.

This is a statutory advocacy service, which means in certain situations people who lack capacity must be referred to an advocate.

An IMCA is not the decision-maker (such as the person's doctor or care manager), but the decision-maker has a duty to take into account the information given by the IMCA.

The *Independent Mental Capacity Advocate (IMCA)* service aims to help particularly vulnerable people who otherwise have no family or friends consult about those decisions.

IMCAs are independent people who work with and support people who lack capacity, and represent their views to those who are working out their best interests.

An IMCA must be instructed, and then consulted, for people who lack capacity and have nobody else to support them (other than paid staff) whenever:

- An NHS body is proposing serious medical treatment
- An NHS body or local authority is proposing to arrange accommodation (or a change of accommodation) in hospital or a care home and (a) the person will stay in hospital longer than 28 days or (b) they will stay in the care home for more than eight weeks

An IMCA may be instructed to support someone who lacks capacity to make decisions concerning:

- Care reviews, when nobody else is available to be consulted
- Adult protection cases, whether or not family, friends or others are involved

Independent Advocates under the Care Act

The IMCA service is not the only form of independent advocacy available to support individuals. New advocacy provision was introduced as part of the Care Act 2014.

The Care Act introduced new <u>statutory advocacy</u> from April 2015. This is for people who have substantial difficulty in being involved with the assessment of their needs, or with their care planning or care reviews, if they have nobody appropriate to help them be engaged. Your local authority can provide more information.

Advocacy and Mental Health

The *Mental Health Act* introduced statutory advocacy for people who are detained under the Mental Health Act or who are under a Community Treatment Order (CTO). This form of advocacy is provided by advocates called *Independent Mental Health Advocates* (IMHAs).

TASK 19

> Conduct some independent research in your area. What advocacy services are available and what service user groups do they help?

TASK 19 (Continued)

TASK 20

Think of an (anonymous) service user in your setting who has used an advocacy service. From the perspective of the service user – was there a favourable outcome? If you are unable to complete this task about a service user, refer back to Task 18 and continue:

TASK 21

Do you consider that there is adequate advocacy provision in your area? Explain your findings.

TASK 22

Summarise your care setting's policy and procedures regarding advocacy provision. (If this is not set out in a separate policy, you may find the information in other policies.)

References

Advocacy Code of Practice

Care Act 2014 Briefing. Clements. L. 2014

Care Act 2014. HM Government.

Chesnay, M. and Anderson, B. (2011) – Caring for the Vulnerable. Jones and Bartlett. London.

http://www.actionforadvocacy.org.uk/

http://www.batias.com/wp-content/uploads/2012/03/New-Advocacy-Charter.pdf

https://en.oxforddictionaries.com/definition/advocacy

https://www.merriam-webster.com/dictionary/advocate

http://www.nhs.uk/Conditions/social-care-and-support-guide/Pages/advocacy-services.aspx

National Institute for Health Research, School for Social Care Research, NHS. Department of Health's NIHR School for Social Care Research.2013.

Ross, D. (2004) – Advocacy. Cambridge University Press. Cambridge.

SSCR Advocacy Scoping Review. 2014

NOTES

NOTES

NOTES

NOTES

NOTES

NOTES

Printed in Great Britain
by Amazon